COMPLETE GUIDE TO FISHING

The Sport Fisherman's Cookbook

COMPLETE GUIDE TO FISHING

The Sport Fisherman's Cookbook

MASON CREST PUBLISHERS, INC.

COMPLETE GUIDE TO FISHING – **The Sport Fisherman's Cookbook**
has been originated, produced and designed by AB Nordbok,
Gothenburg, Sweden.

Publisher
Gunnar Stenmar

Editorial chief
Anders Walberg

Design, setting & photowork:
Reproman AB, Gothenburg, Sweden

Translator:
Jon van Leuven

Nordbok would like to express sincere thanks to all
persons and companies who have contributed in
different ways to the production of this book.

World copyright © 2002
Nordbok International,
P.O.Box 7095,
SE-402 32 Gothenburg, Sweden.

Published in the United States by
Mason Crest Publishers, Inc.
370 Reed Road, Broomall, PA 19008
(866) MCP-BOOK (toll free)
www.masoncrest.com

First printing
1 2 3 4 5 6 7 8 9 10
Library of Congress Cataloging-in-Publication Data on file at
the Library of Congress

ISBN 1-59084-497-1

Printed and bound in Jordan 2002

Contents

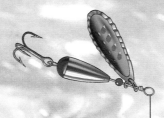

Preface

Cooking your catch outdoors over a campfire or at home in the kitchen is without doubt one of the finest endings a fishing adventure can offer. With its enormous variety of tastes and textures, fish is a fantastic raw material suited to brilliantly simple methods of outdoor cooking and elegant presentations from the kitchen at home. But it is also a sensitive product that demands proper treatment all the way from the water to the frying pan; a fish that is handled correctly gives the person who catches it a degree of gastronomic pleasure equal to the pleasure of the contest itself.

From the high seas into the frying pan

Fish is not only good for you. It also tastes good, as well as offering a wide range of different recipes. A skilled chef can transform any fish into a wonderful gastronomic and culinary experience, but you can quite easily prepare your own fish dish straight after the catch. In other words, fish is a very flexible ingredient both for novices in the kitchen, and for culinary experts. Whether you cook your catch at the waterfront or in the boat shed or if you decide to take the fish home to prepare a dish in your fully fitted kitchen, fish offers you an ocean of wonderful recipes. It is however very important to handle the catch in the correct manner from the moment the fish has been hooked until the prepared meat is placed in the frying pan.

Unfortunately many anglers are more than careless when cleaning and preparing their catch.

KILLING AND CLEANING YOUR CATCH

Firstly, it is important to kill the fish as soon as possible after the catch to prevent excessive suffering, but also to reduce the levels of lactic acid. Fish that are allowed to die a natural death after being hooked become very stressed as they fight to survive, which leads to increased lactic acid accumulating in the meat, thereby affecting both its texture and flavor.

A good way to kill larger fish is to cut off the throat artery by inserting a knife under the gill cover and making a cut towards the abdominal cavity beyond the gill attachment. In this way, the fish dies quickly and is also bled at the same time.

Pressing a sharp knife into the brain, which is located behind the eyes, can easily kill smaller fish. If done correctly the fish dies immediately. Another option is to club the fish in the head with a hard object, for example, a knife handle or a modified mallet. The fish dies immediately.

It is also important to clean the fish as soon as possible after the catch to prevent the spread of putrefactive bacteria from the guts and stomach to the abdominal area and into the fish meat. Cut open the belly from the head to the anal vent or vice versa. Remove the entrails taking care not to damage the gall bladder, the intestines or stomach to

prevent the spread of bacteria. After gutting, rinse the fish in clean water and scrape out the blood vein that runs along the backbone.

Scale fish as soon as possible after catching them, as the scales are easier to remove at this time, before gutting them. Scrape off the scales working from the tail towards the head. Fresh water used to rinse cleaned fish normally contains more bacteria than salt water. It is recommended to pat dry the fish with a clean cloth as it maintains a higher level of quality. The fish can be rinsed later on at home.

STORAGE

Fish is often more sensitive compared to animal meats. Fish meat can, as a result, easily spoil after the catch, especially at air temperatures exceeding $15°C$. The basis for this is that fish have adapted to an environment, which maintains significantly lower temperatures compared to air temperatures, especially during the summer months.

Fish meat spoils quickly on land as it has to cope with an entirely different bacterial flora and also has to take into account the process of self-combustion (autolysis). Self-combustion occurs when enzymes in the fish meat break down cellular tissues once the fish has been killed. This process accelerates in warmer environments. Extensive self-combustion has occurred if the bones in the fish easily loosen from the meat or if the meat becomes loose and tasteless.

Bacterial growth can be avoided and the self-combustion process delayed if the fish is stored correctly. This primarily means cold storage – in a fridge during the summer – if the fish are not taken home right after being caught. Prevent bacterial growth by rubbing the gutted fish with vinegar or salt; thus, salt is very practical to have on any fishing trip. However, excess salt can dry out the meat as it removes water. Vinegar is consequently a better choice.

Fish should be stored in a dry and cool place and never in direct sunlight. Certain fish species e.g. salmon trout and Arctic chars benefit from being wrapped in clean paper or, better still, a clean dry cloth. Grass or even twigs can be used to wrap fish in. On the whole, it is important to leave space around the wrapped fish for air to circulate. For this

reason, try to keep fish separate from each other when in storage. Woven baskets can readily be used to store smaller fish when out fishing. Larger fish such as salmon and trout are normally hung on a tree branch, or the like, to allow them to hang free and be aired, as well as letting them bleed completely.

Storing fish in plastic bags or other airtight bags is a very effective way of spoiling your catch, as is placing the fish in direct sunlight or, even worse, in the boot of your car on a hot day. It goes without saying that gutted fish should be kept off the ground as it contains an extensive bacterial flora.

FREEZING
Fish should be frozen whole, particularly species of high-fat fish. In this way, the fish meat is exposed to reduced levels of bacteria and other impurities, thereby delaying the spoiling process. High-fat fish species such as salmon, salmon trout, Arctic char and eel have normally a shelf life of 3 to 4 months in the freezer, while cod, pike, zander (pikeperch) and other leaner species can be stored in a freezer for at least 6 months. Store all fish in airtight packages in a freezer (at least -18°C). If you do not have access to a vacuum sealer, try to remove as much air as possible from each package by sucking out the air in the package before closing it. Wrapping the fish in aluminum freezer wrap, especially if the fish are stored individually, can also extend the shelf life. Make sure you clearly label each package with details of the fish and date of freezing.

COOKING FISH
Fish that have been handled correctly can be stored in a fridge for a day without freezing them. There are a number of ways to monitor the quality of the fish meat to make sure it is fresh. Check that the fish is still rigid and maintains its original pinkish-red colour, e.g. the red gills. It should be firm to the touch if you press it lightly with one finger, where the meat is elastic and the skin springs back. Obviously the fish should also smell fresh.

There are a number of simple rules to follow when you cook fish. Fish weighing up to two kilograms are ideal for frying, barbecuing and grilling. Larger fish should be boiled or oven baked. High-fat fish such as trout, salmon

and eel are ideal for smoking, in contrast to the meat in many leaner species that dries out if smoked.

Certain fish species, among others pike, can be boiled with their scales after the skin has first been rubbed with one tablespoon of vinegar and/or one tablespoon of salt per kilo of fish and left to draw for 30 minutes (a proven method that improves both the taste and the consistency of all fish meats) and then rinsed and dried to remove the slime. This also removes the characteristic taste of cooked fish, which many find unsavory.

It is not always necessary to use newly caught fish, if you intend to fry. A general rule of thumb is that leaner fish species are normally fried (with butter). In the case of high-fat fish species, such as trout, grilling or barbecuing is recommended. Imagine grilling your newly caught fish over a campfire on a warm summer evening by the sea.

SMOKING FISH
Smoking, which retards bacterial growth and considerably delays the spontaneous combustion process, as well as conserving the fish meat, requires access to some type of smoke. You can choose from either hot or cold smoking. Hot smoking takes only a few hours and requires only a basic smoking process, for example a barrel on a fire, while the cold smoking process takes days to complete using a fixed device containing cooling channels.

Prior to smoking, the fish must be salted by either rubbing salt into the entire fish or brining it in a cure containing herbs and salt. The fish is rinsed in cold water after three to four hours and then allowed to dry for a couple of hours in an airy and cool location.

Smaller fish, which are ideal for hot smoking, are usually hung up by their heads during the smoking process. Larger fish can be smoked by either removing the head, cutting up the belly along the backbone, dividing the fish into two fillet-like halves, removing the backbone and inserting two or more sharp sticks through the meat or simply filleting the fish and smoking them one by one.

A top temperature of approx. 65°C is required when hot-smoking fish. However, the process is started at a low temperature and is gradually increased. The entire process takes between 2 and 10 hours, depending on the size of the fish and the smoking flavor you wish to achieve.

Skinning flatfish

1. First remove the fins and head. Keep the tail fin, if any. It may be used as a "handle". The entrails can be removed by pulling off the head, after first making an incision from the back of the head to the fish's mouth.

2. Make an incision across the tail of the fish as close to the skin as possible using a sharp knife.

3. Pull off the skin. There are a number of ways to do this. One is to pull back the skin using a kitchen towel or twist the skin around the blade of a knife. Use flat pliers, if it is hard to remove the skin.

Smokers are normally fuelled by wood chips from deciduous plants or branches from coniferous plants. It must be pointed out however that different woods result in different smoking tastes. Try different woods and smoking times until you find a smoking flavor that suits you.

A hot-smoked fish has a shelf life of about one week, if it is kept cool. Storing the fish in a freezer will significantly increase the shelf life.

In the cold smoking process, the smoke is led through a long channel before it reaches the fish. The temperature of the smoke, when it comes in contact with the fish, should be much lower compared to hot smoking, i.e. preferably 28°C, but never more than 35°C. Cold smoking requires a fixed smoker that may be rather advanced, yet follows the same rules for fuelling and flavoring as for hot smoking. In most cases, large fish that require cold smoking, e.g. salmon, are sent to a professional curing house. In other words, hot smoking can be considered a do-it-yourself process, while cold smoking, which requires an advanced smoker and specialist know-how, is not everyone's kettle of fish.

Filleting round fish

1. The fish has to be gutted and scaled if required. Do not skin. (Remove, however, any excess skin that may be left since gutting, from the head down to the tail running along one side of the backbone.) Cut down to the backbone behind the head. Holding the knife flat, slide it along the length of the backbone down to the tail, as close to the bone as possible.

2. Detach the fillet.

3. Make a small incision between the skin and the meat at the narrow end of the fillet. Hold the skin and pull it tight. Using a sawing movement, cut away the skin from the fillet. (If you find it hard to hold onto the skin, dip your fingers in salt or use a kitchen towel.)

4. The wider end of a fillet may contain small bones. To obtain a bone-free fillet, cut out the central line until the middle of the fillet. Turn the fish over and repeat as above.

Filleting flatfish

1. First make a cut down to the backbone from the head to the tail fin.

2. Cut against the bones using a sharp knife towards the edge in the direction of the bones. Detach the fillet at the outer edge.

3. Loosen the skin from the fillet by cutting from the narrow end. Cut as close to skin as possible.

4. Cut away the outer edge of the fillet, which is full of small bones. Carry out the same procedure for the remaining fillets. In all, you should have four fillets, if you follow the steps correctly.

Facts about the sportfisherman's catches

SALMON

There are two kinds of salmon, Atlantic and Pacific. Atlantic salmon is the superior of the two, but its taste and appearance can differ depending on when and where it is caught. Salmon is best in spring and summer, and the females are regarded as better eating. I prefer salmon that weighs 6 1/2 to 9 pounds because the fat content is lower. Finest of all is the cultivated Norwegian salmon, with the best-tasting and most tender flesh. The wild Atlantic salmon is longer and narrower; the flesh is redder and not as well marbled.

Baltic salmon belongs to the same species that is caught in the Atlantic. Its flesh is pale because it lives on the fry of Baltic herring and does not ingest carotene from crustaceans. I prefer salmon from other waters because the flesh of Baltic salmon is fattier and looser.

Pacific salmon is not to be compared with Atlantic salmon when it comes to the quality of the flesh. It is drier and the flavor not at all as good.

With salmon, in contrast to many other kinds of fish, there is very little waste. It should be cleaned at once, because the entrails are strongly acidifying and can destroy the flavor of the flesh.

If salmon is bought over the counter, the gills should be pale red and the slime should smell fresh. The blood in the abdomen should be light-colored and dry, and the bones should be firmly attached to the flesh.

RAW SALMON

Raw salmon is a delicacy that requires fresh fish. The best flesh for raw dishes is what is on the backbone when the fish is filleted. It can be scraped off with a spoon and is soft and bland in taste. Otherwise, the flesh from the midsection is used. The texture of the tail section is too hard, and the flesh of the belly is too fatty. Cut the flesh that will be served raw into thin slices, or chop it finely.

SEA TROUT

Sea trout has a lower fat content than salmon and is thus better suited to raw dishes.

It is used in the same dishes as salmon. A fresh sea trout is identified by the same signs as a fresh salmon.

RAINBOW TROUT

Rainbow trout varies greatly in taste depending on where it is farmed and the water it lives in. The flesh is pink, though the color can vary depending on the food the fish gets.

I have encountered broiler-like specimens that were inedible, but if the fish is in good condition and lives free in the ocean, for instance, it is a delicacy. Rainbow trout under 6-1/2 pounds are best for cooking.

PERCH

Perch is a fish that is frequently neglected in cooking but very fit for use if it is filleted properly.

Perch weighing 2 pounds or less are best for cooking. There is most flesh on a perch in late autumn and in spring. Its quality depends largely on the water where it is caught.

A fresh perch is firm in texture, and the eyes are full.

GRAYLING

Grayling has an exaggerated reputation for deteriorating rapidly after it is caught, but it should be cleaned as soon as it is taken.

. The gills should be cut away, and the fish rinsed carefully. It should then be salted immediately, stored in as cool and airy a place as possible, and cooked the same day. It is done when the bones come loose.

A fish under 11 pounds should be filleted in such a way that the backbone remains in one of the halves.

If the grayling is going to be frozen, it should be glazed with ice. Rinse the fish and put it in the freezer. After a few minutes, a film of ice will have formed around it. Take it out, dip it in water, and put it back in the freezer. Repeat this procedure four or five times so there is a protective layer of ice shielding the fish from the air. Put each fish in a plastic bag and freeze.

PIKE

Pike is best during the cold time of the year. The flesh is firm and lean. The hard scales are best removed.

If the fish is to be poached or fried whole, it is fine for the scales to stay on—this helps retain the flavor during cooking. Pike is one of the few fish that tolerate a fairly long cooking time.

Small pike are better to use, because large ones can be tough.

Because the flesh holds together well, pike is good for minced-fish dishes.

A fresh pike should be stiff, with a fresh layer of slime on the surface. The eyes should be full.

CHAR

Char is a perishable fish that should be dealt with as soon as possible after it is caught.

It displays itself to best advantage when newly caught and poached, but it can also be prepared the same way as salmon and sea trout.

COD

Cod is lean and the flesh is relatively loose, so a low cooking temperature is called for. The fish is done, regardless of size, when the temperature is 120°F all the way through. This can be both felt and seen, as the fish is lustrous and glassy at first and then becomes somewhat dull and transparent when the proteins start to coagulate. If the fish gets too hot, the flesh becomes white, dry, and solid. Cooking time depends on the size of the fillet and the temperature of the fish when it goes into the oven. A good way to check on whether it is done is to take the fish out of the oven and cut through a fillet.

A fresh cod should be stiff, with red gills, a fresh smell, and bright, protruding eyes.

MACKEREL

Mackerel should smell fresh; after it has been stored for a short time, it smells and tastes stale.

A lot of people think that mackerel is best during spring and autumn, when the fat content is highest. I myself prefer the somewhat leaner summer mackerel.

The flesh should be firm and the skin bright and shiny.

WALLEYE

The walleye is a delicacy, with firm, white, extremely delicious flesh. A walleye of 3 1/2 to 4 1/2 pounds is best in the kitchen, and if it is going to be poached whole, it is best for the scales to stay on. This preserves the flavors in the flesh, and the skin is easy to pull off before serving.

Fresh walleye should be stiff, with slime on the gills, a fresh smell, and full eyes.

TUNA

Fresh tuna is a true delicacy and should be prepared with great care, so that it remains pink inside. Over-cooked tuna is one of the most horribly dry experiences you can have in the way of fish.

In fact, fresh tuna is one of those raw materials that tastes best of all raw.

The flesh should smell fresh; if it has stood only a little too long, the flesh acquires a sharp, stale smell.

Equipment for cooking fish on the shore

If you make room for some simple cooking gear in your fishing-bag, your fishing trip can be transformed into a culinary experience by the waterside.

SHARP KNIFE
A good knife is a must, and its importance cannot be emphasized enough.

SEASONINGS
Old fly boxes with many compartments make good spice jars. They are small, and you will have room for a good collection of seasonings. A few excellent examples would be salt, pepper, dried dill, pink pepper, thyme, and a ready-made fish blend.

MARINADE
A marinade heightens and changes the flavor. It consists of seasonings, oil, and an acidic ingredient such as vinegar or wine. The acid together with the seasonings breaks down the cell walls in the flesh, making it more tender.

You can prepare the marinade before the fishing trip and bring it in a bottle. Pour the marinade into a plastic bag. Then put the fish in, press the air out, and seal the bag. Your fish will marinate in thirty minutes when you are cooking outdoors. Dry the marinade off with paper towels before you cook the fish.

ALUMINUM FOIL
With the help of heavy-duty aluminum foil you can manufacture a tight-fitting pressure cooker in no time at all. Cooked like this, in its own juice and steam, the fish is succulent and tasty.

The temperature inside the packet is seldom higher than 195°F. The foil lets the radiant heat of the coals in, but keeps the contact heat out.

BAKING PARCHMENT
Baking parchment can be wrapped around the fish before it is wrapped in foil to be laid on a hot stone or in the coals. Paper towels also work excellently. The paper makes a protective cover that retains the flavors.

GRILL
A grill makes it easier to turn the fish on the coals. There are small grills that clip together with brackets.

SMALL TEFLON PAN
A small Teflon pan is lightweight and slips easily into your backpack.

BREADCRUMB BAG
Fill a plastic bag one-third full with fine, dry breadcrumbs and freshly ground pepper, leaving room to shake the fish in the bag.

BURYING BAG
Mix 2 Tbsp. salt, 3 Tbsp. sugar, and 1 1/2 tsp. white pepper in a plastic bag.

Bury the fish in a double layer of plastic bags and keep it as cool as possible. The best thing to do, if possible, is dig an earth-cooled "pantry" on the shore. A salmon weighing about 2 pounds will be ready in 24 hours.

FLASHLIGHT
A flashlight will help you keep track of your food on late summer evenings.

SMOKING BAG
A heavy-duty aluminum bag filled with alder sawdust and sugar makes an ingeniously simple way to smoke fish. The ingredients are put into the bag, which is then sealed and put on the fire or in the oven. This works best for smaller fish. The bags can be bought at well-equipped fishing stores.

Recipes – Perch

Perch has a very full taste and is therefore suitable for both advanced courses and cooking in the simplest way. The easiest way to cook perch is to wrap it in foil and cook it on coal, seasoned with a little salt. The cooked fish may be eaten with your fingers, and be enhanced by a cold beer.

FILLETS OF PERCH STUFFED WITH DILL BUTTER

INGREDIENTS
 fillets of perch
 1 bunch of dill
 ca 2 oz (50 g) butter per person
 salt
 freshly ground pepper
 a few tablespoons of white wine

EQUIPMENT REQUIRED: aluminum foil

SERVED WITH: Boiled potatoes

Grease the foil with butter. Put the salted and peppered fillets on the foil. Put a lot of finely chopped dill and a big knob of butter on top. Sprinkle a few tablespoons of white wine over the fish.

 Close the foil carefully and put in the oven at 390°F (200°C) for 20 minutes. Remove the fillets from the foil and serve with the melted butter. Press the boiled potatoes through a coarse-meshed sieve.

FRIED PERCH FILLETS WITH CHANTERELLES AND SPINACH SALAD

INGREDIENTS
 5 dl (2 cups) small chanterelles
 1 tablespoon minced onion
 2 tablespoons butter
 200 g (8 oz) fresh spinach
1 tablespoon rapeseed oil
 1/2 tablespoon white
 wine vinegar
 salt and pepper
 about 400 g (14 oz) skinless and boneless perch fillets
 1/2 dl (3 1/2 tablespoons) flour
 1 teaspoon salt
 1/8 teaspoon pepper

There are those who just do not appreciate large catches of perch. The easiest way to deal with this fish is to gut and rinse it well, then bake at 200 °C (400 °F) for 20-30 minutes. Cool slightly then remove skin and bones. It is delicious in salad, soup and other dishes. This recipe, however, uses raw perch fillets.

PREPARATION TIME: 30 minutes

SERVING SUGGESTION: Garnish with lemon wedges and parsley.
 Clean mushrooms and sauté with onion in butter until all liquid has evaporated and they begin to sizzle.
 Rinse spinach, removing any large stalks.
 Dry, then shred. Whisk oil, vinegar, and spices and pour over spinach. Toss, then arrange on four individual plates.
 Dip fillets in flour seasoned with salt and pepper.
 Fry in butter until golden, about 2 minutes per side.
 Arrange fish on spinach with chanterelles all around.

Fried perch fillets with chanterelles and spinach salad.

GRILLED PERCH ON A BED OF MANGOLD AND ARUGULA WITH BEETS AND HORSERADISH

INGREDIENTS
    2 beets
    juice of 2 lemons
    1 dl (scant 1/2 cup) of rapeseed or corn oil
    salt and pepper
    100 g (3 1/2 oz) horseradish
    1 tablespoon cornstarch oil
    400 g (14 oz) boneless perch fillet, scaled but skin-on
    100 g (3 1/2 oz) arugula
    100 g (3 1/2 oz mangold
    or 200 g (7 oz) mixed delicate salad greens

Peel and thinly slice beets with a cheese plane. Combine lemon juice, oil, salt and pepper and pour over beets. Marinate at least 1 hour. Cut 3/4 of the horseradish into matchstick pieces; toss in cornstarch and deepfry until golden brown. Salt lightly.

Grill fish, skin side down, in a hot grill pan. Turn and grill until heated through. Heat some of the marinade. Grate remaining horseradish and toss with arugula and-mangold. Drizzle with marinade. Divide the salad among individual serving plates. Top with fish. Garnish with beets and fried horseradish.

BEVERAGE SUGGESTION: A dry white wine or, even better, a fresh rose from the south of France goes well with this perch on its bed of summer vegetables.

OVEN-BAKED PERCH WITH SALT

INGREDIENTS
    2-4 lbs. (1-2kg) sea salt
    small, gutted perch

SERVED WITH: Boiled potatoes and dill butter or fried onions and a chive/tomato salad.

Gut the perch, remove the gills (the red under the lids of the gills, which has a bitter taste), leave the head, and dry with kitchen paper. Cover the perch completely with salt and cook in the oven at 437°F (225°C) for 40 minutes. Dig the fish out of the salt and serve with melted dill butter and boiled potatoes. Can also be served with fried onion rings or a chive and tomato salad.

PERCH HASH

This dish is equally good hot or cold. To go with the perch, feel free to use whatever vegetables are available.

INGREDIENTS:
    1-1/3 lbs. filleted perch
    1 red bell pepper
    1 yellow onion
    1 yellow pepper
    1 medium zucchini
       or other squash
    1 red onion
    4 cloves garlic
    olive oil
    salt
    pepper

Cut out the row of bones in the middle of the fillets. Then cut the flesh into small cubes.

Peel the peppers with a potato peeler and cut out the core of seeds in the squash and peppers. Cut all the vegetables into small cubes.

Pour a generous amount of olive oil into a skillet and carefully sauté the vegetables until they are tender but still crisp.

Add the pieces of perch and shake the skillet. Sauté for about one minute more. Season with salt and pepper.

CLEAR PERCH SOUP

INGREDIENTS
    fillets of perch or whole, small, scaled perch
    4-5 potatoes
    1 very finely chopped onion
    Stock:
    fish bones
    2-3 onions
    2-3 bay leaves
    two allspice corns
    5-8 white peppercorns
    water

SERVED WITH: Toasted Finnish rye bread made with sourdough, 5 1/2 oz (150 g) butter, dill.

Put the bones of the perch in a pan with the spices and the onion. Cover with water. Simmer for 45 minutes and sieve.

(If you cannot or do not want to fillet the perch, remove the gills and innards and put the fish in the hot stock together with the spices. Let them draw for about 30 minutes. The meat from the perch can be added to the ready made soup.)

Peel the potatoes and cut into fingertip-sized cubes. Melt half of the butter, add the onion and fry until golden.

Add the potato cubes and let them sizzle with the onions.

Add the perch stock and simmer until the potatoes are almost done.

Add the pieces of perch and simmer for another little while.

Sprinkle finely chopped dill over and put one slice of toasted and buttered rye bread on top of the soup.

Recipes – Pike

Many people fear all the bones in the pike and therefore avoid eating it. They miss out on a wonderful fish with a mild, unusual taste. Pike can be served as a weekday dinner or as a dinner party course. For festive arrangements it is lovely served with a dry white Bourgogne wine. The brave drink a red Pinot Noir with the pike buns.

PIKE QUENELLES
WITH SPINACH AND A CHEESE SAUCE

    14 oz (400 g) of pike fillets
    1 tbs salt
    10 oz (3 dl) cream
    1 egg
    ground nutmeg
    coarsely ground white pepper
    finely ground lemon peel
    7 1/2 oz (500 g) fresh leaf spinach or 4 oz (250 g) frozen
    2-3 1/2 fl oz (1/2 to 1 dl) white wine

    Cheese sauce:
    19 fl oz (5 dl) milk
    1 1/2 oz (40 g) wheat flour
    1 1/2 oz (40 g) butter
    2-3 1/2 oz (1-2 dl) grated cheese

EQUIPMENT REQUIRED: aluminum foil

Cut the pike into finger-thick shreds, flavor with salt and pepper and mix in ground nutmeg. Mix in a food processor to an even, firm mixture. Add first the egg yoke, then the white. Make sure that everything is properly mixed. Pour the cream in little by little, so that the mixture stays firm. Leave it in a cold place for a couple of hours.

Form egg-shaped quenelles of the mixture with a spoon and put the quenelles on an ovenproof dish. Sprinkle with white wine. Cover with foil and put in the oven at 347°F (175°C) for 15-20 minutes.

Finely shred the spinach and sizzle in a pan. Serve with the quenelles.

Cheese sauce: Melt the butter and add the flour. Add hot milk and whisk. Let it simmer for around ten minutes, while stirring constantly. When the sauce is thick and shiny, season with salt and add the grated cheese. Bring to the boil and serve with the pike quenelles.

FRIED PIKE MEDALLIONS
WITH POTATOES AND A MUSTARD CREAM SAUCE

    1 cleaned and scaled pike
    3 1/2-4 fl oz (11/2 dl) cream per person
    1 tbs dry mustard (with a little sugar)
    3 1/2 fl oz (1 dl) white wine
    finely chopped dill
    finely chopped chives
    coarsely ground black pepper
    salt
    wheat flour
    butter for frying
    2 peeled potatoes/person. Preferably firm potatoes.

Cut the pike into 1 inch (2 cm) thick slices and season with salt and pepper. Sprinkle wheat flour over. Fry the medallions in butter. Pour out the excess butter from the pan. Pour in cream and white wine and season with mustard. Leave to simmer on the stove or put the pan in the oven at 437°F (225°C) for 10-15 minutes.

Boil the potatoes and slice them into thin slices. Put them in an ovenproof dish or on an ovenproof plate. Place the fish on top.

Cook the sauce in the pan until it thickens and add the chives and the dill. Use a lot of herbs. Pour the sauce over the fish.

PIKE BURGERS

INGREDIENTS
500 g (1 1/4 lb) skinless and boneless pike fillets
125 g (4 oz) salt pork
125 g (4 oz) smoked bacon
1 onion
1 egg
1 dl (1/2 cup) whipping cream
    grated nutmeg
    lemon pepper
    1/2 teaspoon salt
    1/4 teaspoon white pepper
    butter

The combination of pork and freshwater fish can be found in many older cookbooks. In the olden days, people used what they had and often paired fatty pork with lean fish.

PREPARATION TIME: About one hour
SERVING SUGGESTION: Serve with riced potatoes, melted butter and carrots or peas.

Rinse fish, removing any small bones. Remove rind from pork and cut into small strips. Peel onion and cut into wedges.

Grind fish, pork and onion in a meat grinder or food processor.

Stir in egg, cream and spices. Fry a small sample and taste. Adjust seasoning, if necessary.

Form into 8 burgers and fry on both sides in butter over medium heat until golden.

BEVERAGE SUGGESTION: A semi-dry white wine, preferably a German Riesling is good with this dish. Or why not a light beer with moderate to full bitterness?

PIKE ON A BED OF POTATOES AU GRATIN

INGREDIENTS:
    ca 2 lbs. (1 kg) peeled firm potatoes
    3 onions
    ca 7 fl oz (500 ml) dry cider
    8 crushed corns of allspice
    some freshly ground black pepper
    10 oz (3 dl) crème fraiche
    1 bunch of finely chopped chives
    1 bunch of finely chopped parsley
    1 young pike ca 3 lbs. (1 1/2 kg) or 18-21 oz
       (500-600 g), filleted

SERVED WITH: Pickled beet

Slice the potatoes. Cut the onion into thin rings. Put the potatoes, onions and mix of spices in layers in a greased, ovenproof dish. Pour the cider over the mixture and put in the oven at 356º F (180º C) for ca 40 minutes.

When the potatoes are done put the cleaned fillets of pike or the cleaned sliced fish on top of the potatoes. Cover with crème fraiche and herbs. Put back in the oven for another 15 minutes. Serve with pickled beet.

POACHED PIKE WITH HORSERADISH SAUCE, CARROTS AND PIKE ROE

Pike has a remarkable flavor and is among the fish valued most highly by the French, who often use it for small pike quenelles. In Scandinavia it is often served poached with grated horseradish and melted butter.

    INGREDIENTS:
    1 roe-filled pike of about 4 1/2 lbs.
    4 carrots
    a piece of horseradish
    2-3 bay leaves
    6-8 whole allspice
    7/8 cup heavy cream
    flour
    butter
    salt
    pepper
    1/2 tsp. 12% vinegar

PREPARATION:
    1. Start by skinning the pike carefully. Then gut it, taking particular care that the egg sacs remain whole. Fillet the pike and cut into beautiful pieces.
    2. Clean the roe, salt lightly and refrigerate for several hours. Peel the carrots and cut into long thin slices. Boil them in lightly salted water until tender but still crisp. Grate the horseradish finely.
    3. Bring about a pint of water to a boil with salt, pepper, bay leaves and allspice. Let the fillets simmer in the water for about 10 minutes. Remove the pieces of fish and keep them warm.
    4. Heat 1-2 Tbsp. butter with 1/2 tsp. flour, adding the cream and a little of the fish broth. Let the mixture cook down into a smooth sauce and season with salt, pepper, 1/2 tsp. vinegar and about 2 Tbsp. grated horseradish.

TO SERVE: Accompany the pike with hot carrots in butter, horseradish sauce, pike roe, some more finely grated horseradish, and boiled potatoes. A couple of tablespoons of melted butter will further heighten the flavor.

Poached pike with horseradish sauce, carrots and pike roe

Recipes – Pikeperch

Pikeperch with egg sauce is a kitchen classic – home cooking at its best. There are many other good fish recipes where pikeperch fits perfectly. The mild fish flavor easily absorbs and carries most accompaniments very well. Serve with a wine that does not drown the flavor of the fish, perhaps a white Bordeaux.

GRILLED PIKEPERCH WITH MUSHROOM SAUCE

INGREDIENTS:
 17-20 oz (500-600 g) scaled fillets of pikeperch with or
 without the skin
 11 oz (300 g) fresh cep mushrooms
 1 finely sliced onion
 10 fl oz (3 dl) créme fraiche
 freshly ground black pepper
 a couple of twigs of rosemary
 (or a few pinches of dried rosemary)
 salt
 butter
 a couple of tbs of white wine

SERVED WITH: Boiled potatoes

Clean the mushrooms and cut them into fingertip-sized cubes. Let the onion sizzle in butter, add the mushrooms and leave to sizzle for a few minutes. Add the crème fraiche and simmer for 3-4 minutes. Season with salt and pepper and add a few twigs of rosemary to give a nice aroma to the sauce.

Heat a frying pan. It has to be very hot. Sprinkle in a little salt and put in the fish fillet. If the fillet has skin, leave the skin-side up. Turn over after ca 30 seconds.

(This phase can be left out.)

Put the fillets on a greased oven tray with a few knobs of butter on the fish and sprinkle the white wine over. Cook in the oven at 392° F (200° C) for around ten minutes.

Serve with the mushroom sauce and boiled potatoes. Sprinkle the dish with some fresh, finely chopped rosemary.

PIKEPERCH WITH HERBS AND GRATED BREAD

INGREDIENTS:
 18-21 1/2 oz (500-600 g) pike-perch fillets without skin
 parsley, basil, thyme, rosemary
 5 1/2 oz (150g) butter
 7 oz (2 dl) grated bread
 7 fl oz (2 dl) white wine
 freshly ground black pepper, salt

SERVED WITH: Boiled potatoes, parsley butter

Season the fillets with salt and pepper and rub some of the butter on the fish. Mix the grated bread and the finely chopped herbs in a food processor (use herbs according to taste).

Sprinkle the grated bread over the fillets of pikeperch and put them in a grated ovenproof dish. Sprinkle the white wine over and put in the oven at 356° F (180° C) for 10-15 minutes.

Pour the liquid into a pan, bring to the boil and whisk in the rest of the butter. (Add perhaps a touch of sugar and a little French mustard.) Serve with boiled potatoes that have been turned in a little parsley butter.

BOILED PIKEPERCH WITH EGG SAUCE

INGREDIENTS
   1-1 1/2 lbs. (500-600 g) whole scaled pike-perch in
      slices, or fillets of pike-perch without skin
   2-3 bay leaves
   4-5 corns of white pepper
   coarse sea salt
   sprigs of parsley
   1 twig of thyme
   1 small piece of leek
   1-2 carrots

SERVED WITH: Potatoes

Egg sauce:
   3 hard boiled eggs
   13 1/2 fl oz (4 dl) milk
   ca 2 oz (50 g) wheat flour
   ca 2 oz (50 g) butter
   10 sprigs of parsley

Put the vegetables and the spices in water and boil for a little while. Remove from the stove and add pieces of pike-perch cut into thick slices. Leave the fish in the warm stock for 10-20 minutes depending on the thickness. Remove them and serve with potatoes, egg sauce and perhaps also melted butter.

Egg sauce: Melt the butter in a pan. Add the flour and let it sizzle while stirring. Pour in the hot milk, little by little, while stirring. Leave to simmer for 10-15 minutes, add the finely chopped eggs and the finely chopped parsley.

Boiled pikeperch with egg sauce

Recipes – Burbot

Burbot has a firm and white meat that goes with almost anything. It is at its best when served with mild sauces, such as the classic white sauce. It is served with a relatively dry white Bordeaux wine.

FINE FISH PUDDING WITH BURBOT
(SERVES AT LEAST 6)

INGREDIENTS:
    7 oz (2 dl) grains of rice
    18 oz (500 g) of burbot fillets
    1 small leek
    3 eggs
    3 1/2 fl oz (1 dl) cream
    3 1/2 oz (1 dl) frozen green peas

SERVED WITH: Melted butter, potatoes, broccoli and tomato salad.

Boil the rice until almost soft and let it go cold.
    Remove the bones and cut the fillets of burbot into small pieces.
    Parboil the leek, cut into rings. This can be done beforehand.
    Whisk the eggs slightly and mix in the other ingredients. Pour into a well-greased oval dish with a thin layer of breadcrumbs. Cook in the oven for 30 minutes at 347°F (175°C). Serve with melted butter and freshly boiled potatoes. Cooked broccoli or a tomato salad goes well with this dish.

BURBOT FRICASSEE

Burbot can be difficult to prepare, so many choose other fish. Buy skinless and boneless fillets and enjoy this interesting fish. Actually almost any kind of fish can be used in this recipe.

INGREDIENTS
    2 dl (3/4 cup) water
    1 fish bouillon cube

1 small fennel bulb
1 small leek
2 dl (3/4 cup)
créme fraiche or whipping cream
400 g (14 oz)
chanterelles or
other mushrooms
600 g (1 1/3 lb) skinless and boneless burbot fillets
chopped chives
chopped parsley

PREPARATION TIME: About 30 minutes

SERVING SUGGESTION: Serve with rice or potatoes.

    In a sauté pan, heat water and add bouillon cube. Shred fennel and leek. Simmer in bouillon until tender. Whisk in créme fraiche. In another pan, saute mushrooms without added fat until all liquid has evaporated. Transfer to saute pan. Cut fish into 1 cm (1/2") thick chunks and add. Simmer until cooked through, about 5 minutes. Sprinkle with chives and parsley and serve directly from the pan.

BEVERAGE SUGGESTION: A dry white wine is good with this tasty fish fricassee. Choose a young Chardonnay.

FRIED BURBOT ON A BED OF ROOT VEGETABLES
WITH MELTED GARLIC CHEESE

INGREDIENTS
    ca 4 1/2 oz (150 g) filleted burbot per person
    breadcrumbs
    garlic cheese

SERVED WITH:
    9-11 oz (250-300 g) potatoes per person
    root celery
    carrots
    parsnip
    viper's grass
    one knob of butter for frying

2 tbs of white wine vinegar
salt and pepper
lemon
parsley

Shred the potatoes and root vegetables into coarse match-shaped sticks. Put the butter in a pan and let it melt without changing color. Put in the vegetables and let them sweat. Add a drop of white wine vinegar, salt and pepper.

Turn the burbot around in breadcrumbs and fry at medium heat. When they are warm, put knobs of garlic cheese on top and finish frying.

Serve on a plate with the fish on top of the vegetables. Decorate with lemon and parsley.

Burbot fricassee

Fried burbot on a bed of root vegetables with melted garlic cheese

Recipes – Grayling

Grayling is seldom found in the supermarket due to its short shelf life. If you have caught grayling, however, you can expect a delicacy. Be careful not to over-season grayling – it already has a natural taste of thyme. If you do not want to eat it straightaway, grayling profits from being marinated.

GRAYLING SCRAMBLER

INGREDIENTS:
   one whole grayling, ca 2-3 lbs. (1 1/2 kg)
   1 yellow onion
   2 cooking apples
   2 tbs butter
   2 tsp salt

Scrambled eggs:
   4 eggs
   8 tbs cream, milk or water
   salt and pepper
   a little butter

Open the grayling, gut it and rinse thoroughly. Leave the head.

Fill the cavity with finely chopped onion and apple. Put the fish in foil and put knobs of butter and a lot of salt on it. Close the foil and put the packet on hot coals or in the oven at 392°F (200°C) for 4 minutes on each side.

Melt the butter in a pan. Whisk the eggs slightly and pour them over the liquid in the pan. Stir carefully over low heat until the eggs have stabilized.

DEVILISH GRAYLING

INGREDIENTS:
   3 lbs. (1.5 kg) filleted grayling (a whole fish)
   1 red onion
   1/2 tsp salt
   1/2 tsp ground white pepper
   3 1/2 fl oz (1 dl) cream per person
   1 tbs French mustard per person

SERVED WITH:
   ca 2 lbs. (1 kg) new potatoes
   dill

Mix the cream, mustard and chopped red onion and let it simmer together for a few minutes. Put in the filleted and seasoned fish and let everything simmer together for 10 minutes. The time may vary depending on the size of the fish. Serve with boiled potatoes and dill.

GRAYLING WITH JUNIPER

INGREDIENTS:
   1 lb. (1/2 kg) of grayling per person
   1-2 tbs salt
   a few twigs of juniper with ripe berries
   finely chopped yellow onion
   2 cooking apples
   3 1/2 oz (100 g) butter

Chop the twigs with the berries finely. Mix it with finely chopped onion, salt, chopped apple and butter. Stuff the grayling. Put on glowing coal for around 5 minutes on each side.

FLYFISHERMAN'S GRAYLING

INGREDIENTS:
   one whole, fresh grayling, ca 3 lbs. (1.5 kg)
   1 1/2 tbs salt per liter of water
   water

Creamy porridge:
   semolina
   thick cream
   salt
   sugar
   (when served as a dessert, a little cinnamon and sugar)

Gut the grayling and boil it whole in slightly salted water.

The grayling's own flavor of thyme will be the only seasoning. The fish is done when the meat easily comes off the bones. This will take 30-35 minutes.

Serve with creamy porridge, which can also be had as a dessert. Creamy porridge is made from semolina without sugar, made with cream instead of milk. (See cooking instructions on the packet.) The porridge can also be served as a dessert with a little cinnamon and sugar.

Fly-fisherman's grayling

Recipes – Eel

The blood of the eel is poisonous, but the poison evaporates during cooking. The eel is of great gastronomic value and has been enjoyed in Scandinavia since the Iron Age – the remains of eel have been found at archaeological diggings from that period. Today, eel is mostly eaten smoked, but why not try something else? Eel is well worth discovering. Yes, it is fat, but if that is what keeps you away from it just try it in moderation!

EEL CASSEROLE PIRI PIRI

INGREDIENTS:
 2 lbs. (1 kg) skinned fresh eel
 1 small leek
 1 red and 1 green pepper
 2 cloves of garlic
 1/3 tsp piri piri (very hot spice)
 2 tbs butter or oil
 3 1/2 fl oz (1 dl) white wine
 7 fl oz (2 dl) cream
 3 1/2 fl oz (1 dl) créme fraiche
 3 1/2 fl oz (1 dl) chopped parsley

SERVED WITH: Bread

Cut and rinse the eel into 1 inch (2.5 cm) long pieces. Chop the leek, peppers and garlic finely and let it all simmer with the fat with a little piri piri in a sauté pan. Add the eel, pour the wine and cream over and let it simmer for 10-12 minutes. Put everything in a greased, ovenproof dish and put crème fraiche on top. Leave in the oven at 482°F (250°C) until slightly golden. Sprinkle parsley on top and serve with fresh bread.

SPICY EEL

INGREDIENTS
 one whole fresh eel, ca 2 lbs. (1 kg)
 1 red onion
 2 carrots
 1 3/4 pints (1 liter) fresh, parboiled funnel chanterelle or champignon (field) mushrooms
 1 tbs wheat flour
 3 1/2 fl oz (1dl) red wine
 3 1/2 fl oz (1dl) water
 hot mango chutney
 black pepper
 Tabasco sauce

SERVED WITH: Pasta (or boiled potatoes pressed through a sieve)

Cut the eel into pieces about 1 inch (2.5 cm) long. Quickly fry them in a sauté pan together with finely chopped red onion, carrots and funnel chanterelle or champignon mushrooms.

Powder the flour over and add 3 1/2 fl oz (1 dl) of red wine and water – enough to barely cover. Flavor with a little hot mango chutney, black pepper and Tabasco.

Serve with pasta or boiled potatoes pressed through a sieve.

COOKED EEL
WITH LEMON AND LEMON GRASS

INGREDIENTS:
 one eel ca 2 lbs. (1 kg)
 1 1/2 tbs salt per liter water
 10 whole corns of white pepper
 the juice of one lemon
 3 tbs butter
 2 tbs flour
 stock
 lemon grass

SERVED WITH: Boiled potatoes

Scrape and rinse the skinned eel. Remove all the blood. Leave the eel in running cold water for a while.

Boil a lot of water together with salt, white pepper corns and lemon juice.

Put the eel in the water and let it boil for 15 minutes.

Take the pan off the heat and pour 10 fl oz (3 dl) of the liquid through a sieve.

Make a roux of 3 tbs butter and 2 tbs flour. Thin down with stock until it is suitably thick.

Add finely chopped lemon grass.

Serve with boiled potatoes.

Cooked eel with lemon and lemongrass

Recipes – Arctic Char

Arctic char has a firm and fine meat that is suitable for boiling. Just like other "salmon fish" Arctic char can be pickled raw. It is relatively fatty and can therefore be grilled or fried on coal. With raw pickled Arctic char it is nice to drink a flowery, somewhat spicy white wine like Oregon Pinot Gris for example.

**ARCTIC CHAR
WITH ANCHOVY AND CRÉME FRAICHE**

INGREDIENTS
one Arctic char, ca 3 1/2 oz (3 hg) per person or 2-3 lbs. (1-1.5 kg)
1 pint (2.5 l) water
3 1/2 fl oz (1 dl) red wine vinegar
1 large carrot
1 large onion
3 bay leaves
1 1/2 oz (0.5 dl) salt
a few sprigs of dill

Sauce:
1 jar of créme fraiche
3 anchovy fillets
1 bunch of dill
salt and pepper

SERVED WITH: Boiled potatoes and the anchovy sauce or a hollandaise/dill and mayonnaise sauce

Clean the Arctic char. Boil in a lot of water seasoned with red wine vinegar, onion, bay leaves and salt. Leave to simmer for ca 15 minutes. Add the fish and poach until the backbone just comes off (around 12 minutes, depending on the size of the fish).
    Chop the anchovy fillets and mix with the rest of the ingredients for the sauce. Leave in a cool place for at least one hour before serving.
    Serve the Arctic char with boiled potatoes and the anchovy sauce or, alternatively, a hollandaise or dill and mayonnaise sauce.

**GRILLED ARCTIC CHAR
WITH BLEAK ROE AND CRÉME FRAICHE**

INGREDIENTS:
fillets of Arctic char ca 5 1/2 oz (150 g) per person
créme fraiche
1 tbs bleak roe
red onion
fresh dill, salt and pepper

SERVED WITH: Boiled potatoes pressed through a sieve, dill, lemon.

Mix the créme fraiche with the bleak roe, finely chopped dill, finely chopped red onion, salt and pepper.
    Quickly grill the fillets of Arctic char on a grilling pan or a frying pan, preferably in olive oil. Season with salt and pepper.

ARCTIC CHAR IN THE OVEN

INGREDIENTS:
1 whole, cleaned small Arctic char per person
finely chopped funnel chanterelle mushrooms
finely chopped leek
1 bunch of finely chopped dill
3 1/2 fl oz (1 dl) white wine
3 1/2 fl oz (1 dl) creamy milk
butter and breadcrumbs

Put the Arctic char on a well-greased ovenproof dish, covered in breadcrumbs. Leave in the oven at 437° F (225° C) for around 5 minutes.
    Remove the fish from the oven and add the finely chopped ingredients. Put back in the oven for another 5 minutes. Pour some white wine and creamy milk on top.
    Back in the oven for yet another 5 minutes, then the dish is ready for serving.

Grilled Arctic char with bleak roe and créme fraiche.

Recipes – Mackerel

Mackerel is a relatively fatty fish, which needs to be handed carefully. Fatty fish go off sooner than other fish, which is why they must not be left in the freezer for too long. Handled in the right way, mackerel tastes heavenly. The distinct taste goes well with other robust flavors. Smoked mackerel and a white Chardonnay are perfect together, and with fried or grilled mackerel a Muscadet is very nice.

FALL MACKEREL WITH HORSERADISH, APPLES AND PARSLEY ROOT

INGREDIENTS:
1 fall mackerel 1-1 1/2 lbs. (500-700 g)
1/2 slice of lemon
1-2 cooking apples
1-2 parsley roots
a generous amount of parsley, preferably wide-leafed
a bit of horseradish
some butter
salt and pepper
oil

SERVED WITH: Mashed potatoes or bread

Fillet the mackerel, keep the skin and put the fish with the skin-side up in a sauté pan with a touch of water, salt and lemon. The liquid should just barely cover the bottom of the pan. Let the fish simmer on low heat under a lid until it is cooked through and the liquid is almost gone.

Peel the parsley roots and apples (remove the pips from the apples).

Chop the parsley coarsely, leave some of the stalk on the leaves.

Cut the parsley roots length-wise and then cut them into 1/2-1 inch (1-2 cm) thick pieces. Cut the apples into segments, about the same size as the parsley roots. Turn the apples over in some butter. Put the parsley roots in a sauté pan with some salt and a touch of water. Boil until soft under a lid. Then add the apples and let everything boil for a few minutes. The liquid should almost disappear.

Flavor with salt and grated horseradish.

Sprinkle some oil over the parsley and gently stir some coarsely grated horseradish and salt by mixing gently with your hand.

Put the apples and parsley roots in a warm dish with the parsley and serve beside the cooked mackerel fillets.

Serve with mashed potatoes or nice fresh bread.

MACKEREL WITH BALSAMIC-MARINATED PEARL ONIONS

INGREDIENTS
2-4 mackerel
2 tbs oil for frying
30-40 pearl onions
4 tbs coarsely chopped tarragon
4 tbs good olive oil
4-6 tbs balsamic vinegar
salt and freshly ground pepper

SERVED WITH: potatoes and raw or boiled cauliflower

Gut and fillet the mackerel, leave the skin, and put to one side.

Chop the tarragon and mix with oil and vinegar. Season with salt and pepper.

Peel the pearl onions. Boil in salted water. Remove from the water and let them drain thoroughly. Carefully heat the marinade (this can be prepared earlier).

Fry the mackerel only on the skin-side until it is just about cooked through. Put the fish on warm plates or serving dish with the skin-side up. Season with salt.

Put the warm pearl onions and some of the marinade on top, or arrange on a serving dish.

Serve with boiled potatoes and cauliflower.

Mackerel with balsamic-marinated pear onions

Recipes – Plaice

The classic plaice dish is a fried plaice with butter and lemon, but there are many ways that it can be served. If you wish to fry plaice it should be put on ice for a day after the catch, or it will curl upwards in the frying pan. A mild Bordeaux wine that does not compete with the unobtrusive plaice goes well with this fish.

FILLETS OF PLAICE
BAKED IN MANGOLD (WHITE BEET)

INGREDIENTS:
  2 plaice 1 1/2 lb. (750 g)
  1 medium sized mangold
  1 lemon
  2 shallots
  2 segments of garlic
  3 1/2 fl oz (25 cl) of cream
  1 tbs coarse mustard
  3/4 oz (25 g) butter
  olive oil
  salt and pepper

Fillet the plaice and double over the thin end, so that the fillet has the same thickness throughout.

Season with salt and pepper and sprinkle over the peel of one lemon, finely chopped shallots and garlic.

Remove the stalk from the white beet and rinse it. Quickly dip the leaves in boiling water and then put them beside each other on kitchen paper.

Cut the stalks and sauté them in olive oil until soft. Add cream and leave it to cook into a thick, creamy sauce. Season with salt, pepper and lemon juice.

Let the sauce cool and pour it over the fillets, which should be packed inside the leaves of the white beet.

Put the packets on an ovenproof dish that has been greased with butter.

Bake, swept in foil, in the oven at 347° F (175° C) for around 25 minutes.

Serve straight from the ovenproof dish.

FRIED PLAICE

INGREDIENTS
  2-2 1/2 lbs. (1-1, 2 kg) plaice
  1 tsp salt
  1/3 tsp ground white pepper
  3 tbs butter
  3 tbs breadcrumbs
  2 yellow onions
  4 tbs capers
  4 pickled beets
  1 lemon
  parsley

SERVED WITH: 2 lbs. (1 kg) boiled potatoes

Remove the head of the plaice and gut it thoroughly. Leave the skin, but cut a cross on the thick part (so that the cooking time will be the same for the whole fish).

Turn the fish in breadcrumbs, sprinkle with salt and pepper. Fry in butter in the oven at 347°F (175°C) for ca 30 minutes, the white side turned down.

When the fish is almost done add finely chopped onion and, five minutes later, capers and the beets.

Put the plaice on a serving dish and pour the onion and caper mix on top. Garnish with lemon and parsley. Serve with boiled potatoes.

The dish can be varied by serving it with shredded bacon and finely chopped pickled gherkins, which adds to the slightly sour taste that is demanded by this recipe.

PLAICE IN WHITE WINE SAUCE

INGREDIENTS
White wine sauce:
2 dl (3/4 cup) vegetable
bouillon
2 dl (3/4 cup) white wine
3 dl 1 1/4 cups)
whipping cream
1 teaspoon salt
1 teaspoon cumin
1/2 teaspoon ground ginger
2 teaspoons cornstarch stirred into 1 tablespoon
    cold water.

Fish:
1 medium leek, trimmed and sliced
8 plaice fillets
8 slices bacon
40 g (1/3 cup) grated parmesan cheese

Fish: bacon and onion are a familiar combination in the
modern kitchen. The seasoning in this sauce is unusual
for fish.

PREPARATION TIME: About 50 minutes

OVEN TEMPERATURE: 200°C (400°F)

SERVED WITH: new potatoes and tiny peas.

In a saucepan, combine fish stock and wine, and reduce
over high heat until about 2 dl (3/4 cup) remains. Add
cream and simmer until slightly thickened, about 35 minutes. Add seasonings.
    Remove from heat. Add cornstarch mixture and cook
until thickened.
    Grease an ovenproof dish. Sprinkle sliced leek over the
bottom.
    Bake 10 minutes. Roll up fish fillets, inside out, and
wrap each in bacon. Arrange on leeks. Stir cheese into
sauce and pour over fish.
    Bake 20 minutes.

Plaice in white wine sauce

BEVERAGE SUGGESTION: The trendy seasoning of the
fish is good with a modern, fruity "new world" white
wine. Try a Sauvignon Blanc or Chenin Blanc from South
Africa.

WINE AND CREAM-COOKED PLAICE

INGREDIENTS
    one plaice 2-2 1/2 lbs. (1-1.3 kg)
    1 tsp salt
    1 leek
    3 carrots
    1 small leaf celery
    7 fl oz (2 dl) white wine
    3 1/2 fl oz (1 dl) cream
    pepper
    basil

SERVED WITH: Boiled potatoes pressed through a sieve

Put the gutted, skinned and salted plaice on a bed of leek
and shredded carrots and celery in a small roasting pan.
    Pour over white wine (it should reach over the bottom
end of the fish). Poach under a lid of foil in the oven at
347° F (175° C) for ca 5 minutes. Remove the foil and add
3 1/2 fl oz (1 dl) of cream. Let this boil without lid until
thickened. Season with salt, pepper and some basil.

Recipes – Cod, Haddock & Whiting

Cod is the most important saltwater fish. It is so common that it has gained an unfair reputation of being boring. It is, however, a splendid base for a nice meal and tastes best when cooked in a simple way as soon as possible after catching. Why not try slicing it and boil in slightly salted water? In Norway, red wine is often served with a casserole of cod, which is a sensation of flavors for those who are used to drinking white wine with fish. Try a red Pinot Noir with cod the next time!

COD (HADDOCK OR WHITING) IN LEMON AND HERB SAUCE

INGREDIENTS
   ca 1 3/4 lbs. (3/4 kg) skinned fillet of cod
      (haddock or whiting)
   7 fl oz (3 dl) water
   1 cube of fish stock
   2 tbs freshly pressed lemon juice
   1 tsp salt
   2 twigs of thyme
   2 twigs of tarragon
   2 egg yokes
   3 1/2 fl oz (1 dl) cream
   2 tbs chopped thyme, tarragon and parsley

SERVED WITH: boiled potatoes, vegetables

Cut the fillets into portion-sized pieces. Bring water to the boil together with the stock cube, lemon juice, salt, thyme and tarragon. Put in the fish and let it simmer gently for around four minutes, until done. Remove it and keep it warm by wrapping it in aluminum foil. Sieve the fish stock and let it boil for a little while. Whisk the egg yokes slightly. Together with the cream, pour into the stock. Heat the sauce until it thickens, do not let it boil. Add the chopped herbs and season with salt.
   Serve with the sauce, boiled potatoes and vegetables.

PRINCE-FISH

INGREDIENTS
   ca 1 3/4 lbs. (3/4 kg) skinned fillets of cod
   1 tsp salt
   17 fl oz (5 dl) water
   1 tsp white wine vinegar

Sauce:
   2 tbs butter
   7 fl oz (2 dl) fish stock
   2 egg yokes
   salt
   1 tbs wheat flour
   10 fl oz (3 dl) cream
   2 tbs sherry

SERVED WITH: Lobster or shrimp and green asparagus, boiled potatoes

Cut the fillets of fish into portion-sized pieces. Boil water with salt and vinegar and poach the fish for around four minutes until it is almost done. Sieve off the fish stock. Remove the fish and keep it warm by wrapping it in foil so that it does not go dry, and leave it in the oven at 167 ° F (75° C).
   Make a white sauce of butter and flour, add the fish stock and cream and let it simmer for at least 5 minutes. Whisk the egg yokes slightly with sherry and add to the sauce, do not let it boil. Season with salt.

COD PROVENÇALE (HADDOCK OR WHITING)

INGREDIENTS:
   ca 1 3/4 lbs. (3/4 kg) skinned fillets of cod, haddock or
   whiting
   2 tbs freshly pressed lemon juice
   1-2 cloves of garlic onion
   1 green pepper, shredded
   7 oz (200g) sliced champignon mushrooms
   1 cube fish stock

Cod Provençale (haddock or whiting).

    2 tbs olive oil
    1 tsp salt
    3 sliced tomatoes
    1 tbs chopped parsley
    7 fl oz (2 dl) water

SERVED WITH: Rice or potatoes, salad

Cut the fish into portion-sized pieces. Mix the oil, lemon juice, salt and garlic. Turn the fish over in the mix. Put the fish, onions, slices of tomatoes, parsley, peppers and champignons in layers an ovenproof dish. Dissolve the stock cube in water and pour over. Put a lid on the dish or cover with aluminum foil and bake in the oven at 347° F (175° C) for 20-25 minutes.
    Serve with rice or potatoes and a salad.

COD WITH BACON AND LEEK

This recipe is originally from Gullholmen. Restaurateur Bengt Petersen brought it to a course at Gerlesborg School.

That's when Meta Bruto adopted it and gave it a modern touch with bacon and leek.

INGREDIENTS:
    600 g (1 1/3) lb) thick cod fillets, skin on
    3 tablespoons coarse salt
    150 g (5 oz) sliced bacon
    1 medium leek
    2 tablespoons chopped parsley

PREPARATION TIME: About 30 minutes plus two hours in the refrigerator

SERVING SUGGESTION: Serve with boiled potatoes.
    Sprinkle fish with salt. Cover with plastic wrap and refrigerate about 2 hours. Rinse off salt, then simmer in water to cover for about 8 minutes.
    While fish is cooking, fry bacon until crisp.
    Clean and slice leek.
    Sauté until soft.
    Arrange fish on a serving platter. Top with bacon and leeks.
    Sprinkle with parsley.

Cod with bacon and leek

BEVERAGE SUGGESTION: Cod is a flavorful fish, and when served in this manner, a medium-bodied red wine with moderate tannin is the best choice. Select a lighter red Bordeaux or a red wine from the Loire valley or northern Italy. Serve lightly.

HADDOCK WITH OCEAN CRAYFISH

INGREDIENTS
   4 large haddock fillets,
   700-800 g (1 1/2 -1 3/4 lb)
   2 dl (1/4 cup) crayfish or fish stock
   2 dl (1/4 cup) beer
   1 kg (2 1/4 lb) potatoes
   2 parsnips, about 150 g (5 oz)
   2 dl (1/4 cup) coffee cream or half and half
   salt and pepper
   4 tablespoons (1/4 cup) capers
   4 tablespoons (1/4 cup) chopped pickled beets
   unsalted butter
   dill fronds
   4 cooked ocean crayfish

Many feel that haddock is a more refined fish than cod. It is even better when served "English-style" and garnished with whole crayfish.

PREPARATION TIME: About 45 minutes

OVEN TEMPERATURE: 175° C (350° F)
Roll up fillets and place in a greased ovenproof dish. Add stock and beer to cover. Boil potatoes and parsnips and mash. Add cream as desired. Season with salt and pepper.
   Bake until fish is opaque, about 20 minutes.
   Spoon a mound of vegetable puré onto each plate. Top with fish.
   Sauté capers and beets in a generous amount of butter and pour over fish.
   Garnish with dill fronds and crayfish.

BEVERAGE SUGGESTION: This classic fish dish can be served with a light beer or a dry white wine.

GOTHENBURG-STYLE WHITING

INGREDIENTS
   1 bunch parsley
   20 small whiting
   1 1/2 tablespoons butter
   2 tablespoons flour
   2 dl (1/4 cup) fish stock
   1 dl (1/2 cup) white wine
   1 dl (1/2 cup)
   whipping cream

This dish is a Gothenburg specialty. It is served to adults with patience and a side dish for skin and bones.

PREPARATION TIME: 35 minutes

SERVING SUGGESTION: Serve with boiled potatoes.

Coarsely chop parsley and blanch in boiling water for a few seconds.
   Clean fish, cutting off heads and tails. Rinse thoroughly.

Simmer fish in lightly salted water to cover for 5-10 minutes, according to size.

Remove from cooking water and keep warm.

Melt butter, stir in flour and slowly add fish stock, wine and cream.

Simmer until thick. Stir in chopped parsley.

BEVERAGE SUGGESTION: Whiting has a very mild, nutty flavor. For that reason, any beverage should not be too dominating. A light, fresh and dry white wine from Italy or a cool Pilsner are the best choices.

STUFFED FILLETS OF WHITING

8 fillets of whiting, skinned
2 tbs cod's roe

3 1/2 oz (100 g) cleaned, coarsely chopped shrimp
2 tbs chopped dill
1/3 tsp white pepper
the juice of 1 lime
7 fl oz (2 dl) water
4-5 tbs of spreadable shrimp cheese
salt and pepper

SERVED WITH: Boiled potatoes, salad

Spread the roe, shrimp and dill on the fillets and roll them up. Sprinkle with pepper.

Bring the water and lime juice to the boil. Put the rolls in with the opening downwards and let them boil for around five minutes, until done.

Remove the fish. Bring the stock to the boil and whisk in the shrimp cheese. Season with salt and pepper and pour it over the fish. Serve with potatoes and a salad.

Recipes – Trout

Sometimes, in the context of food, trout is called by its German name, "forelle". This sounds delicious, and the trout is indeed a fantastic fish to cook. It is most exquisite when cooked straight after being caught, but can be kept for two to three months in the freezer if you want. When it has been frozen for at least two weeks the fish can be pickled raw.

**WARM-SMOKED TROUT
WITH APPLES AND ROE OF SALMON
(SERVES CA 10)**

INGREDIENTS
   1 warm-smoked trout ca 2 lbs. (1 kg)
   3 Belle de Boskop apples (or other large, sour cooking
     apples)
   1 tbs butter
   3 1/2 fl oz (1 dl) white wine or Noilly Prat
   ca 1 oz (25 g) salmon roe per person
   salt and freshly ground white pepper

SERVED WITH: Soured cream (7 fl oz (2 dl) cream and the juice of 1/4 lemon) or crème fraiche, fennel, dill, toasted white bread

Remove the skin and bones from the trout. Put the gutted fish meat in a bowl. Avoid the fat meat around the abdomen.

   Peel the apples and cut them into small segments. Heat them in butter and let them go slightly brown. Pour in some white wine and let them simmer until soft, without going mushy. This will not take long.

   Carefully mix in the warm-smoked salmon with the apples. (If the food will not be served straight away, leave the apples to cool first.) Season with salt and a generous amount of pepper. Mix in half of the roe and distribute among small, round dishes.

   When serving, the dishes can be turned over and the rest of the roe added on top of the trout-mix.

Serve with soured cream and paper-thin slices of raw fennel seasoned with a little salt and dill just before serving, and toasted bread.

(The warm-smoked trout tastes the most when eaten straight after being smoked, without having been kept in the refrigerator. If you wish to make the dish in advance, you can, however, keep it in the refrigerator over night.)

TROUT TARTARE

INGREDIENTS:
   4 boned trouts with skin
   11 oz (300 g) fillets of trout
   3 fillets of anchovy
   6 corns of green pepper
   1 pickled, salted gherkin
   1 tbs capers
   3 egg yokes
   some salt
   2 tbs olive oil
   1/2 fl oz (2 cl) cognac
   1 splash of Worcester sauce
   1 splash of Tabasco or cayenne pepper

SERVED WITH (per person):
   1 tbs bleak roe
   1 egg yoke
   small, fine lettuce leaves

Mix the fish, spices, olive oil and cognac in a food processor or mixer, alternatively chop everything finely and mix. Add the egg yoke and capers. Season. Garnish with bleak roe and egg yoke. Leave cold for an hour or two before serving, to let the flavors grow.

ENDIVES WITH HERB-SAUTÉ, GRILLED TROUT AND BAKED VIPER'S GRASS

INGREDIENTS
4 boned trout with skin

SERVED WITH:
4 endives (chicory)
1/4 lemon
vegetables; e.g. 1 carrot, 1 small zucchini, 1 root of
   parsley, 1 onion and 2 tbs chopped, fresh tarragon
ca 10 viper's grass
ca 5 fl oz (11/2 dl) cream
some butter
salt and freshly ground white pepper
some mustard

Cook the endives until tender in slightly salted water with some lemon. Let them drain properly.

Chop the vegetables in a food processor or with a vegetable chopper. Gently fry them in a casserole dish and add a little water, let them simmer until soft. Season with salt, pepper and chopped tarragon. Add the endives and put on a lid. Keep warm.

Peel the viper's grass. Cut them and boil them in a little water and cream until soft and the cream is boiled in. Season with salt and pepper.

Spread them out in a greased, ovenproof dish and put a few tablespoons of whisked cream on top mixed with some mustard, and sprinkle with lemon juice. Put in the oven at grill temperature until there is a light crust on top.

Grill the trout with the skin-side down in a grill-pan, so that the heat slowly goes up through the skin. When the top of the fish is warm, the fish is done. Remove the fish from the pan, season with salt and pepper and put it on a warm plate with the skin-side turned up.

Serve with the gratin.

No sauce is needed, but some lemon is nice with the fish.

Recipes – Salmon

The best dishes with salmon are the ones that are the easiest to cook – for example, the grilled salmon below. You can also stuff the cleaned and gutted fish with dill, wrap it in foil and bake it on coal. A well-chilled beer is delicious with these recipes.

SALMON CARPACCIO WITH AVOCADO

INGREDIENTS:
    22 oz (600 g) fresh skin-free fillet of salmon
    the juice of one lime or 1/2 lemon
    4 tsp olive oil
    1 tsp salt
    2 tsp rosé pepper
    1 ripe avocado
    dill

Put the fillet of salmon in the freezer for at least 24 hours. Then cut it into leaf-thin slices and arrange these on the plates. Sprinkle over lime juice and oil, salt and rosé pepper.

    Cut the avocado in half, remove the pip and peel the fruit. Cut the fruit meat into boat-shaped slices and arrange them beside the salmon, together with dill.

    Serve the salmon immediately. It must not be left in the lime juice for any longer than it takes to prepare the avocado. If left any longer, the flavor and consistency will deteriorate.

SALMON POACHED COLD

INGREDIENTS:
    ca 1 1/2 lbs. (3/4 kg) skin-free fillets of salmon

    Liquid:
    13 1/2 fl oz (4 dl) water
    1 tbs salt
    13 1/2 fl oz (4 dl) white wine vinegar
    200g brown sugar
    1 tsp whole cloves
    1 tsp whole corns of white pepper
    1 tsp coarsely ground fresh ginger

SERVED WITH: Boiled potatoes, cucumber salad

Cut the salmon into 1/4 inch (1/2 cm) thick slices. Mix all the ingredients for the liquid and bring to the boil. Let it simmer for 10 minutes. Add the slices of salmon and simmer gently for another 3-4 minutes. Let the fish cool in the liquid.

    Serve the fish cold with cucumber salad and boiled potatoes.

DANDELION SALMON IN A PRESSURE COOKER

With the help of aluminum foil you can make a "pressure cooker" in which the fish will be steamed in a few minutes.

INGREDIENTS:
    4 pieces of salmon (or other fish) of 5-7 oz. each
    an armful of tender dandelion leaves
    pink pepper
    salt
    scant 1/2 cup water or wine
    4 sheets of aluminum foil

Dandelion salmon in pressure cooker

PREPARATION

1. Parboil the dandelion leaves in a little salted water. Fold the aluminum foil in half to make a double layer. Place a piece of fish on top of each one and sprinkle with pink pepper and salt. Distribute the dandelion leaves over the salmon.

2. Fold the foil so that it is closed on three sides. Add the water or wine through the open side. Close the packet so that it is completely sealed.

3. Put the "pressure cooker" on hot stone or directly in the fire. The packet will now puff up into a ball.

4. After 4-5 minutes the fish is done.

To serve: Cut a cross in the "ball" and serve at once with soft whipped potatoes or boiled new potatoes.

BUTTERFLY SALMON WITH PARSLEY BUTTER-SAUCE

INGREDIENTS:
   ca 1 1/2 lbs. (700 g) skin-free fillets of salmon
   1 1/2 tsp salt
   7 fl oz (2 dl) water

Parsley butter-sauce:
   1 bunch of curled parsley
   water
   1 finely chopped shallot
   3 1/2 fl oz (1 dl) dry white wine
   3 1/2 fl oz (1 dl) fish stock
   ca 5 1/2 oz (150 g) butter (preferably unsalted)
   salt and white pepper

SERVED WITH: Boiled potatoes, cucumber salad

Start with the sauce. Parboil the parsley in boiling water for 1 minute. Put it in cold water straight away. Shake off the water and chop it finely.

Boil the shallot with the wine until almost all of the liquid has steamed off. Add the fish stock and let it soak in until 1 fl oz (1/3 dl) is left. Add the butter in small portions. The sauce must not boil after the butter has been stirred in – it will be too thin if that is done. Season with salt and pepper and stir in the parsley just before serving. Keep the sauce warm.

Cut the fillet into four equal pieces. Cut almost all the way through each piece and separate the parts, so that it looks like a butterfly. Salt the fish and boil in a small amount of water for around 5 minutes in a sauté pan without a lid.

Serve the salmon with the sauce and boiled potatoes, and perhaps a cucumber salad.

BAKED FILLET OF SALMON WITH JERUSALEM ARTICHOKE SAUCE, MUSHROOMS AND POTATOES

INGREDIENTS
   1 1/3 lbs. filleted salmon with skin
   some grains of coarse salt

Sauce:
   1 lb. Jerusalem artichokes
   2 1/2 cups chicken bouillon
   1 2/3 cups heavy cream
   salt
   pepper

Vegetables:
   7 oz. fresh mushrooms, one or more of any kind
   6 shallots
   4 potatoes
   2 oz. flat-leaf parsley
   salt

PREPARATION:

1. Peel the Jerusalem artichokes and boil in the chicken bullion until soft. Add the heavy cream. Blend in a blender and strain through a sieve. Add salt and pepper.

2. Divide the salmon fillet into four parts and sprinkle with a few grains of coarse salt. Bake in a 350°F oven for about 10 minutes.

3. Clean and slice the mushrooms. Peel and slice the shallots and potatoes. Chop the parsley. Sauté the potatoes and shallots in butter. Add the mushrooms and continue frying until they are golden brown. Add the chopped parsley.

To serve: Place the fish on a bed of vegetables. Heat the sauce and pour over.

GRILLED SALMON

   ca 22 oz (600 g) fillets of salmon
   1 tbs oil
   1 tbs sweet sherry
   1 tbs soy sauce

SERVED WITH: Salad, potatoes or bread

Cut the fish into four equally sized pieces. Mix oil, sherry and soy sauce and brush the fish with the mix. Fry the fish on a charcoal grill, in an electric grill or in a grilling pan, 3-4 minutes on each side.

Recipes - others

GRILLED OCEAN CATFISH WITH SPRING VEGETABLES

FOUR SERVINGS
8 almond potatoes
2 black salsify
2 celery stalks
Sauce:
10 spring onions
2 carrots
40 g(1 1/2 oz) fresh ginger
8 dl (3 1/3 cups) chicken stock
50 g (3 tablespoons)
unsalted butter
salt and pepper
1 beet
corn oil
4 skinless and boneless ocean catfish fillets, about 80 g
(3 oz) each

Ocean catfish is an especially "meaty" fish. Other kinds of fish can be used in this recipe, even lamb and chicken.

PREPARATION TIME: One hour

Clean potatoes and cut in half lengthwise.

Peel and halve black salsify (place in acidulated water after peeling). Cut celery into 5 cm (2") lengths. Blanch vegetables in salted water.

Halve spring onions lengthwise. Peel and grate carrots and ginger. In a saucepan, sauté ginger and onions in a little butter until soft. Add stock and carrot. Reduce over low heat until half the original amount remains. Whisk in butter and season with salt and pepper. Pour into a food processor and puré until smooth. Strain.

Peel and shred beet. Heat oil to 175° C (350° F).

Deep-fry until crisp.

BEVERAGE SUGGESTION: The hearty fish and silky black salsify (one of wine's best friends) go well with a medium-bodied red wine or a more flavorful dry white wine.

LIGHTLY GRILLED TUNA

A simple dish, where the tuna harmonizes beautifully with a simple salad.

INGREDIENTS:
1 1/2 lb tuna fillet
3-4 Tbsp olive oil
salt
pepper

Salad:
4-5 tomatoes
1/2 sliced red onion
1/2 peeled cucumber
1 Tbsp. capers
10-15 olives
8 anchovy fillets
mixed salad greens
Red wine vinaigrette:
1/4 cup red wine vinegar
1/2 cup olive or other oil
salt
freshly ground white pepper

For garnish:
coarsely chopped basil

PREPARATION:

1. Blanch, peel and seed the tomatoes, then slice. Cut the cucumber into small pieces. Combine cucumber and tomatoes with the other salad ingredients.

2. To make the vinaigrette, first dissolve the salt in the vinegar. Add the remaining ingredients and stir.

3. Cut the tuna into pieces and paint with olive oil. Sprinkle with salt and pepper. Grill the fish very quickly in a hot grill pan.

To serve: Sprinkle the tuna with coarsely chopped basil and serve with the salad.

BAKED FISH WITH ASPARAGUS AND HERBS

This dish generally suits any catch.

INGREDIENTS:

4 skinless fish fillets of about 6 oz. apiece
1 lb. trimmed green asparagus
1 2/3 – 2 1/2 cup chopped mixed herbs, such as parsley, basil and chives
7/8 cup heavy cream
7/8 cup fish bullion
3 Tbsp butter
2 finely chopped shallots
2 egg yolks
salt
freshly ground white pepper

PREPARATION:

1. Set the oven at 300° F and place the fillets on buttered plates.

2. Cut the asparagus into 1 1/4 inch pieces. Heat the shallots in a little butter without letting them color. Add the heavy cream and fish bouillon and cook the mixture down until it has thickened into a light, creamy sauce. Season with salt and pepper.

3. Bake the fish on the plates for about 8-10 minutes. Meanwhile, boil the asparagus in lightly salted water for 2-3 minutes and drain in a colander.

Baked fish with asparagus and herbs

4. Heat the sauce and pour into a blender. Add the egg yolks and blend into a light, fluffy sauce. Pour the sauce back into a saucepan and heat carefully, stirring constantly, without letting it boil, to make a thick, creamy sauce. Fold in the asparagus and chopped herbs.

To serve: Set the fish out on four heated plates and spoon the asparagus and herbs over it. Serve with mashed potatoes.

POACHED SPINY DOGFISH
STUFFED WITH CRAYFISH AND SPINACH

INGREDIENTS:
    70 g (2 1/2 oz) salmon fillet
    20 crayfish tails
    1 teaspoon tomato paste
    2 egg yolks
    1 dl (1/2 cup) whipping cream
    1/2 teaspoon salt
    2 tablespoons minced onion
    1 dl (1/2 cup) blanched spinach butter
    400 g (14 oz) spiny dogfish or shark fillets (preferably 4
    fillets)

Potatoes:
    6 boiled potatoes
    1 small carrot
    2 garlic cloves
    1/2 onion
    1/2 red onion
    1/2 fennel bulb
    100 g (3 oz} sun-dried tomatoes in oil
    1/2 g (pinch) saffron
    fish stock (bouillon cube)
    salt and pepper

Eggplant chips:
    1 eggplant

Spiny dogfish is a favorite of fish lovers and sportfishermen. This is a luxury recipe, and it demands full attention
for a perfect result.

PREPARATION: About one hour

OVEN TEMPERATURE: 224° C (425° F)

Fish:
Place salmon, crayfish, tomato paste, egg yolks, cream and
salt in a food processor and puree until smooth.
    Sauté onion with spinach in a little butter.
    Split fish fillets horizontally (disregard if very thin).
Open and place on a flat surface. Season with salt and pepper. Arrange spinach on fish. Top with fish puré.
    Fold over edges and roll up. Wrap tightly in plastic
wrap. In a sauté pan, bring a little water to a boil. Add fish
packet, cover and simmer slowly for about 20 minutes.

Potatoes:
Slice potatoes, carrot and garlic. Cut onions and fennel into
wedges.
    Sauté in some oil from the tomatoes. Stir in saffron.
Shred sundried tomatoes and add.
    Add water to almost cover. Add a small amount of fish
stock and salt. Simmer 10-15 minutes. Season with salt and
pepper.

Eggplant chips:
Thinly slice eggplant. Deep-fry until golden. Drain on
paper towels.

BEVERAGE SUGGESTION: A light luxurious wine suits
luxury food. A dry white Bordeaux with class or a Sauvignon Blanc from New Zealand both have the freshness to
match the dogfish and the crayfish. Wine connoisseurs
would perhaps prefer a Sauvignon Blanc from Steiermark
in Austria.

FISH IN PAPER WITH A FOIL JACKET

A recipe that suits most sportfishermen. The good flavors of the fish and seasonings stay inside the paper, giving off a glorious fragrance when the package is opened.

INGREDIENTS
    2 lbs. whole gutted fish
    salt
    pepper
    3 tbsp. butter
    1 cluster flat-leaf parsley
    1 handful cherry leaves
    sandwich paper
    aluminum foil

PREPARATION
    1. Rinse the fish thoroughly and salt and pepper it. Stuff the abdomen with butter, parsley and cherry leaves.
    2. Wrap the fish in a couple of layers of sandwich paper. Then wrap in aluminum foil and seal carefully.
    3. Lay the fish on the coals. Turn often so the juices will run through the fish and baste it.
    4. Open the package after about 45 minutes. Check to see that the flesh comes loose from the backbone.
    To serve: Eat directly out of the wrapping or serve on a platter.

FISH IN CHICKEN WIRE

Use fresh herbs according to their availability. The chicken wire holds the fish together during grilling.

INGREDIENTS:
    1 salmon, walleye, ocean perch or pike weighing about 1 lb.
    at least 1 1/4 cups coarsely chopped mixed herbs, such as lovage, basil and parsley
    chives
    lemon juice
    chicken wire

PREPARATION:
    1. Stuff the fish with the coarsely chopped herbs and chives. Salt the fish inside and out.
    2. Skewer the fish on a long stick and then wrap it in chicken wire. Grill over coals for about 25 minutes, turning frequently.
    3. Open the chicken wire carefully and take the loose fillet portions from the back.
    To serve: Top each fillet with the herb stuffing, sprinkle with cut chives, and squeeze lemon juice over all.

LATE SUMMER FISH STEW

INGREDIENTS
2 large baking potatoes
2 tablespoons olive oil
salt and pepper
2 dl (3/4 cup) fish stock
2 dl (3/4 cup) white wine
2 dl (3/4 cup) crème fraiche or whipping cream
2 g (1/8 teaspoon) saffron
500 g (1 lb) mussels
1 bunch radishes
1 large carrot
2 red onions
200 g (7 oz) monkfish fillets
200 g (7 oz) skinless eel fillets
200 g (/7 oz) spiny dogfish or
shark fillets
2 teaspoons cornstarch stirred into 1 tablespoon
cold water (optional)
chopped chives
lemon wedges

Fish stews are always beautiful and fun to make. Fillets do not add as much flavor as whole fish, but they do save time. The types of fish used in this stew are not always easy to find, but the recipe works well with most kinds of white freshwater and saltwater fish.

PREPARATION TIME: About 45 minutes

OVEN TEMPERATURE: 225°C (425°F)

Brush and rinse potatoes. Cut into large wedges and place on an oiled baking tray. Sprinkle with salt and pepper and drizzle with olive oil. Bake about 20 minutes, turning halfway through. In a saucepan, combine fish stock and wine and reduce over high heat until about half the original amount remains. Add cream and reduce by 1/3. Whisk in créme fraiche and saffron. Season with salt and pepper. Scrub mussels well, discarding any which are open or broken.

Place in a saucepan in a little lightly salted water. Cover and boil until all are opened. Discard any which have not opened.

Clean and trim radishes. Peel carrot, halve lengthwise, then slice thinly. Peel onion and cut into thin wedges.

Cut monkfish diagonally into 1 cm (1/2") slices. Cut eel and dogfish into eight pieces of equal size. Grill monkfish in a hot grill pan. Sauté eel and dogfish on both sides in olive oil.

Sauté vegetables in a deep frying pan, then add dogfish and eel.

Add sauce and bring to a boil. If using additional cream instead of créme fraiche, thicken with cornstarch mixture.

Arrange potatoes and mussels in the bottom of deep plates.

Ladle over fish stew and top with grilled monkfish.
Garnish with chives and lemon wedges.

BEVERAGE SUGGESTION: A fresh, young, dry white wine is good with this fish stew.

LE BIG MAC

A little ordinary respectable tomato ketchup goes well with this fish variation on the world-famous hamburger.

INGREDIENTS:
  1 1/3 lbs. fish fillet
  2 baking potatoes
  1/4 cup olive oil
  3-4 Tbsp. butter
  3 tomatoes
  1/4 lb. fresh spinach
  4 sprigs rosemary
  4 cocktail sticks, for skewers

Pepper salsa:
  1/2 yellow pepper
  1/2 red bell pepper
  1 tomato
  1/2 papaya
  chili sauce
  salt
  pepper

PREPARATION:
  The salsa:
  1. Blanch and skin the tomato and peppers. Remove the seeds and cut the flesh into cubes. Cube the papaya.
  2. Let the cubes soften in a hot skillet with a little oil. Season with chili sauce, pepper, and salt. Set aside.
  3. Set the oven at 390°F.
  Scrub the potatoes. Leaving the skin on, cut each into four slices of equal thickness. Lay them on a cookie sheet covered with baking paper and paint with equal parts olive oil and melted butter. Salt the potatoes and roast in the oven until they are soft.
  4. Cut the fish into eight pieces of equal size. Sauté in butter until golden brown, then sprinkle with salt. Blanch the three tomatoes and cut each into four slices. Clean the spinach and sauté lightly in a little butter.
  5. Take four plates and put a roasted potato slice on each one. Cover the potato with a slice of fish and a little spinach. Add another layer of potato, fish and spinach. Top each burger with three slices of tomato flesh.
  To serve: Skewer the whole burger with a cocktail stick and garnish with rosemary. Spoon the pepper salsa around it.

SANDWICH

This recipe makes 20 beautifully marbled sandwiches.

A sandwich will keep for a week if stored in its wrap in the refrigerator. Excellent for taking along on day trips.

INGREDIENTS
  1 loaf of unsliced white bread, several days old
  1 loaf of unsliced dark rye bread

Herb butter:
  1 cluster of parsley
  1/2 clove garlic
  small piece of leek
  1/2 lb. salted butter

  1/4 lb. cucumber
  2 tsp. salt
  1 tbsp. Dijon mustard
  7 oz. thinly-sliced cold-smoked salmon

PREPARATION
  1. Cut off the top and bottom crusts of the bread. Slice each loaf lengthwise into 4 to 6 slices.

  2. In a blender, mix the parsley, garlic and leek. Add the butter and mix again.

  3. Slice the cucumber thinly and sprinkle with salt. Let stand for 15 minutes. Then place the slices on a towel and carefully wring out all moisture.

  4. Spread the herb butter on a slice of white bread and cover with cucumber slices. Spread the mustard on a dark slice and put slices of salmon on it. Turn these surfaces toward each other. Now put the appropriate filling on the surface of the top slice. Alternating types of bread, continue in the same way until you have a construction consisting of eight (or more) slices of bread. Wrap in sandwich paper, tie it up with string, and wrap the whole package in a damp towel.

  6. Place this packet on a cutting board (so the layers are horizontal) and put another cutting board on top to press the sandwich. Put everything in the refrigerator and let it stand for several hours.
TO SERVE: Open the packet and trim the edges of all four sides. Slice and serve.

LOBSTER SOUP

INGREDIENTS
  shells from 4 lobsters
  1 onion
  1 carrot
  1 parsnip

  2-3 tablespoons tomato paste
  3 dl (1 1/4 cups) whipping cream
  2 1/2 tablespoons cognac
  salt and white pepper

Preheat oven to 200° C (400° F). Crush lobster shells. Cube root vegetables.

Place shells and vegetables on an oven tray and bake 20 minutes. Transfer to a large saucepan. Add water to cover, then simmer 30 minutes. Strain broth into a new saucepan, discarding shells and vegetables. Add cream and reduce until about 1 liter (quart) remains. Just before serving, add cognac, salt and pepper.

Sauces

WHITE SAUCE

2 1/2 tbs wheat flour
17 fl oz (5 dl) milk
1-2 tbs butter
salt and white or black pepper
perhaps a few tbs of cream

Whisk the flour with some of the milk in a pan. Then pour in the rest of the milk. Add the butter and bring to the boil while stirring. Boil on a low heat for nearly 5 minutes. Season with salt, pepper and perhaps a little cream.

HOLLANDAISE SAUCE

5 1/2 oz (150 g) butter
3 egg yokes
3 tbs water or dry white wine
1/2 – 1 tbs lemon juice
1/3 tsp salt, white pepper

Melt the butter and let it cool.
Mix the egg yokes with water or wine in a small pan. (NOTE! If the pan is made of aluminum, the sauce may turn gray if a steel whisk is used.) Place the pan in a water-bath in a larger pan. The water should simmer, not boil. Continue whisking until the sauce has thickened.

Remove the pan from the heat. Add the melted butter while stirring powerfully. Start by adding it drop by drop, then a little more. Avoid creating sediment. If the sauce starts to curdle, add a cube of ice or some ice-cold water and whisk powerfully.

Season with lemon and some salt and pepper.

SALMON SAUCE

3 tbs mustard (or 1 tbs unsweetened)
1 tbs sugar
salt and white pepper
1 tbs vinegar
3 1/2 fl oz (1 dl) oil (3 1/2 fl oz (1 dl) mayonnaise can be used instead of the oil)
3 1/2 fl oz (1 dl) chopped dill

Mix the mustard, sugar, salt, pepper and vinegar in a bowl. Add the oil drop by drop to start with, then a little more, while stirring powerfully. The sauce should be fairly thick and creamy. Mix in the dill.

FISH STOCK

(for ca 25 fl oz (75 cl) ready-made stock)
1-1 1/2 lbs. (500-750 g) fish (e.g. head, bones and fins
  from a large fish)
ca 33 fl oz (1 liter) water
2 tsp salt
1 piece leek or 1 onion cut into segments
dill or parsley

A good way to make the most of small fish or the insides of larger fish is to make a stock from them. The stock can be used as a base for sauces and soups and can be frozen.

Rinse and clean small fish, cut into pieces. If you use a large fish head, the gills should be removed first or the stock will turn bitter.

Put the pieces in a casserole dish, add cold water and slowly bring to the boil. Carefully remove the scum and add salt, onion and dill or parsley. Simmer under a lid on low heat for around 20 minutes. Sieve and taste. The stock can be boiled for another 5 minutes, without a lid.